EYEWITNESS TO THE
TUSKEGEE
AIRMEN

BY MARCIA AMIDON LUSTED

The Child's World®
childsworld.com

Published by The Child's World®
1980 Lookout Drive • Mankato, MN 56003-1705
800-599-READ • www.childsworld.com

Acknowledgments
The Child's World®: Mary Berendes, Publishing Director
Red Line Editorial: Design, editorial direction, and production
Photographs ©: Corbis, cover, 1; U.S. Army Signal Corps/AP Images, 4; U.S. Army/
AP Images, 7; Detroit Publishing Company/Library of Congress, 8; Bettmann/Corbis,
10, 13; Toni Frissell Collection/Library of Congress, 14, 17, 18, 23, 26; Rick Bowmer/
AP Images, 21; Everett Historical/Shutterstock Images, 24; Lev Radin/Shutterstock
Images, 29

ISBN 9781634074209

LCCN 2015946228

Printed in the United States of America
Mankato, MN
December, 2015
PA02281

ABOUT THE AUTHOR

Marcia Amidon Lusted has written more than 100 books and 500 magazine
articles for young readers. She loves to write about history and about the
lives of people who helped change the world.

TABLE OF
CONTENTS

Chapter 1

READY TO SERVE

It was early morning on March 24, 1944. The United States was at war. Together with the other Allied Powers, U.S. troops were fighting Germany, Italy, and Japan. These three countries were part of the Axis Powers.

A group of Allied B-17 **bombers** was traveling to Berlin, Germany. Their target was the Daimler-Benz factory. Daimler-Benz made tanks for the war. The bomber pilots would try to destroy German war equipment. It was a dangerous mission. The bombers were big, heavy planes. Smaller, swifter enemy planes could attack them. German planes swarmed in the clouds, preparing to strike.

But the Allied forces were ready for them. A group of Mustang fighter planes traveled with the bombers. These fighter planes swooped into German airspace. The pilots easily spotted the enemy planes. The nimble Mustangs dipped and dived as they neared their targets. On the cloudy day, the bright red paint on the Mustangs' tails seemed to glow.

The pilots of these Allied fighter planes were a special group. They were known as the Tuskegee Airmen. They were the first black pilots in the U.S. military. These pilots had faced challenges and **prejudice**. But they soon proved their skills. That day, they shot down three powerful German jets. As a result, the Allies' mission was a success. The pilots earned a Distinguished Unit Citation for the all-black 332nd Fighter Group.

Five years earlier, there were no black pilots in the U.S. military. Some Americans doubted black pilots' skills. However, many young black people wanted to serve their country. They were eager to show the world what they could do.

Organizations urged officials to remove the ban on black pilots. Finally, in 1940, the U.S. Army Air Corps began an experiment. The corps would accept black students to flight-training programs. If they did well, they could fly for the U.S. Army.

Applications flooded in from all over the country. However, only four pilot schools would accept black students. The most famous one was the Tuskegee Institute. At the time, Tuskegee was an all-black college. The school worked with the U.S. Army to provide pilot training. In July 1941, the first group of men started training at Tuskegee.

One Tuskegee student was Benjamin O. Davis Jr. He was the son of the first black general in the U.S. Army. Davis had already graduated from West Point, the nation's top military school. But he had always dreamed of becoming a pilot. Davis immediately applied for the Tuskegee program. Known for his deep voice and thoughtful gaze, he quickly became a leader to the other **cadets**.

Davis and the other students had to master many subjects. They took classes in science and radio communication. Cadets learned to predict weather patterns. They pored over maps and interpreted flight plans. Only the best made it to the next stage: advanced flight training.

Benjamin O. Davis Jr. was one of the first black students at ▶ West Point military academy.

▲ **The Tuskegee Institute, where cadets trained, was one of the oldest black colleges in the United States.**

Flight training was the same for black and white cadets. However, the military was **segregated**. The Tuskegee Army Airfield was a separate base for black cadets. At first, this airfield had only a dirt runway. The first training groups took off and landed on bumpy, dusty surfaces. Still, the cadets were determined to succeed. In March 1941, First Lady Eleanor Roosevelt visited the airfield. "These boys are good pilots," Roosevelt wrote. "I had the fun of going up in one of the tiny training planes with the head instructor."[1] No other First Lady had flown in a plane with a black pilot. Pictures of her flight appeared in newspapers. The Tuskegee training program had gotten Americans' attention.

When the cadets began their training, the United States was at peace. Everything changed on December 7, 1941. One cadet, Charles Dryden, was enjoying a day off with his family. Dryden wore his cadet uniform proudly. On his bus ride home, a woman stopped him. "Soldier," she asked, "do you know we're at war?"[2] Dryden stared at her in disbelief. The Japanese navy had just attacked Pearl Harbor in Hawaii.

On December 8, 1941, the U.S. Congress officially declared war on Japan. Days later, the United States declared war on Japan's allies, Germany and Italy.

The Army Air Corps needed good pilots for the war. Soon, the first Tuskegee cadets would graduate. They were ready to fly. But many Americans still doubted black pilots' skills. The cadets waited anxiously. They wondered when they would be able to serve.

Chapter 2

PREPARING FOR WAR

It was a crisp March day in 1942. Benjamin O. Davis Jr. was flying a small plane above Tuskegee Army Airfield. A flight instructor sat next to him, watching Davis operate the controls. The plane landed gently in the airfield. Then the instructor got out of the plane. Davis prepared to take off again—this time on his own. It would be a very special flight.

"This was what I had been waiting for," Davis later said. "Up until this moment, he had watched my every move . . . now . . . it was my airplane."[3] The plane soared into the sky. Other cadets cheered. Davis was the first black pilot to take a solo military flight.

For the cadets, a solo flight was their final test. New trainees were both frightened and excited about this challenge. By April, five black cadets had completed their solo flights. At a special ceremony, they earned their silver wings. They were officially qualified pilots.

Soon, other cadets followed. "My heart was racing so fast," remembered Charles Dryden. "All the hurdles that could have killed my dream were now . . . just history."[4] Colonel Noel Parrish pinned the silver wings on Dryden's cadet uniform. Dryden was ready to fly for the U.S. Army.

By 1943, nearly 1,000 black cadets had earned their wings. But they still faced challenges. People with prejudiced views still doubted that the men would make good pilots. The black cadets would need to prove that they were just as good as white pilots. "We were always trying to be better," said pilot Roscoe Brown.

"We were taught that you had to be better than whites in order to move ahead, so we were very competitive."[5]

By August 1942, there were enough pilots to staff an air **squadron**. The 99th Squadron was the first all-black unit in the Air Corps. Benjamin O. Davis Jr. was the unit's commanding officer. Later, three more squadrons were added. They were all part of the 332nd Fighter Group.

In September, the squadron was placed on alert. The men could be sent to war at any time. But months passed. Pilots waited and waited. Every day, they took practice flights. The men wanted to be ready for **combat**. "We trained and trained," said Clarence Jamison. "The white classes were finishing and [authorities] were sending them to the Pacific, to Europe, because they needed the pilots. But . . . nobody seemed to want us."[7]

> "Prejudice made it a lot tougher for a black fellow to get his wings. It made us the best of the best, and helped to create a strong fighting force."
>
> —Robert Deiz, Tuskegee Airman[6]

▲ **Tuskegee cadets studied maps and navigation plans before their flights.**

Pilots heard many rumors that they would leave soon. Most rumors turned out to be false. Finally, in March 1943, they received their orders. The Tuskegee Airmen would take the train to New York. Then they would board a ship to join the war.

Chapter 3

INTO THE SKIES

In early April 1943, Charles Dryden got off the train at Camp Shanks, New York. He felt proud and excited about going to battle. "I felt a strong sense of being a part of a special group," he recalled.[8] The 99th Squadron boarded the USS *Mariposa* ocean liner. One month later, the squadron had arrived in Morocco.

For their first mission, the Tuskegee Airmen would travel with more experienced pilots. They

◄ Members of the Tuskegee Airmen attended a meeting about a military mission.

would depart from northern Africa. Their aim was to attack Pantelleria, a tiny Italian island. This mission would help the Allies invade Sicily.

Early on June 2, 1943, the Tuskegee pilots got into **formation**. Anxiously, they watched Pantelleria come into view. Airman William Campbell remembered dropping a bomb for the first time. "I was a bit nervous," he said. "We didn't know much about combat flying, but we were all determined to do our best. Dropping the first bomb, however, was just a matter of luck."[9] Campbell watched a more experienced pilot drop a bomb first. Then he carefully fired his own bomb at the target.

Every day, the 99th Squadron pilots flew over Pantelleria. The men nimbly guided their Mustang P-47 planes, firing at enemy targets. The Tuskegee

"Blacks have fought in every war going back to the Revolutionary War. Each time that we did that, we thought that if we defended the country . . . the broader community would end segregation."

—Dr. Roscoe Brown, Tuskegee Airman[10]

15

Airmen had craved experience in combat. Most were pleased with their assignment. "It was the first time any of them ever shot at the enemy," said Benjamin O. Davis Jr. "They gave a good account of themselves . . . and, most important, they all came back safely."[11]

On June 11, the Axis soldiers on the island surrendered. It was a clear victory for the Allies. And it was a victory for the Tuskegee Airmen, too. They had begun to prove their skills. The Tuskegee Airmen began to feel at home on their North Africa base. They flew together and developed close friendships. They also shared missions with white pilots. The airmen were earning the respect of others in the military.

However, after less than a year, it was time to move on. The 99th Squadron was transferred to the coast of Italy. The men prepared for missions from their new base, Ramitelli Airfield.

Benjamin O. Davis Jr. continued to be a leader to the ▶ Tuskegee Airmen after they went overseas.

Chapter 4

THE RED TAILS

I n Africa, the Tuskegee Airmen had often worked with white officers. Their time in Italy was different. Black men and women held all jobs at Ramitelli Airfield. It was a completely segregated area. Four black squadrons, all part of the 332nd Fighter Group, used the base.

Airmen needed to adjust quickly to the unfamiliar location. But soon, they received a welcome surprise. At Ramitelli, airmen would be flying new Mustang P-51 planes. They marveled at the beautiful new machines. These were some of the fastest, most effective planes used during World War II.

The Tuskegee Airmen needed a way to find each other's planes in the sky. The bombers that they protected would also need to identify them. At the base, men found numerous cans of bright red paint. They used this paint on the tails of the new planes. Soon, the airmen had earned the nickname "The Red Tails."

Pilots flew on **air raids** into Czechoslovakia, Austria, and Germany. The Tuskegee pilots protected bombers from enemy aircraft. The Army Air Corps conducted bombing runs during the day. The sunlight helped bombers hit their targets. But it also meant enemy pilots could see the Allied bombers. That's when the Red Tails swooped into action. The Tuskegee pilots bravely fought back against enemy planes. Other pilots called them the "Red-Tailed Angels." They kept the Allied bombers safe.

During one mission, the Tuskegee Airmen were **escorting** an Allied bomber. Suddenly, they were surrounded by enemy aircraft. In just four minutes, the pilots destroyed five enemy

> "Up in the blue it doesn't make any difference where you come from, what color you are. . . . I can appreciate the land, sea, engineers, cooks, nurses, Red Cross, tanks, defense workers, people buying bonds and a thousand and one other things. I look at them and say, 'This is worth fighting for.'"
>
> —*Charles Hall, Tuskegee Airman*[12]

planes. It was a new record. Soon afterward, the Tuskegee pilots met a cluster of German jets. Jets were a new technology. They were much faster than the P-51 Mustangs. But despite their slower speed, the Tuskegee pilots shot down three German jets. German troops started calling them "The Black Birdmen." The Germans were amazed by the Tuskegee pilots' skill.

Another successful mission took place in May 1944. The 99th Squadron attacked Axis troops on Monastery Hill, Italy. German soldiers climbed the hill, ready to attack. Then the Tuskegee Airmen's planes swept in. As the bombs exploded around them, the soldiers scattered and the attack was abandoned. But the airmen

The Tuskegee Airmen earned the nickname "The Red Tails" ▶ from the red paint on their aircraft.

were not finished yet. They also bombed a nearby German fortress, forcing it to surrender.

The Tuskegee Airmen took pride in their work. "They were all long flights, usually five hours," said pilot Charles McGee. "We were glad when . . . we could be less rigid in keeping formation with one another. Fighter **sweeps** were great fun."[13]

During the war, the Tuskegee Airmen shot down 109 Axis fighter aircraft. They destroyed fuel storage facilities, trucks, and trains. The pilots even sank a German patrol boat. During the war, Tuskegee Airmen flew 15,000 flights on 1,500 missions. With every flight, the airmen risked their lives for their country.

Sergeant William Bostic worked in the control tower, directing ▶ the Tuskegee Airmen's takeoffs.

Chapter 5

RETURNING HOME

With their daring flights, the Tuskegee Airmen had earned other pilots' respect. But back home, they still faced prejudice.

During the war, many military officers enjoyed going to officers' clubs. The clubs provided a relaxed atmosphere away from fighting and practice exercises. According to official military policies, these clubs were for all officers. But often, the Tuskegee Airmen were not welcome. In 1945, the 447th Bombardment Group was stationed at Freeman Field in Indiana. There, authorities set up two separate clubs. One was only for white officers. The white officers' club offered comfortable furnishings. A fireplace and a game room provided warmth and activities. Another, smaller club was for black officers. This club had few tables and only coal stoves for heat.

Bill Terry and Coleman Young were airmen with the 447th Bombardment Group. In April 1945, they carefully planned a rebellion. One evening, dozens of black officers inspected each other's clothing. They made sure to meet all uniform rules. In groups of three, the men filed into the white officers' club. Each group of officers politely asked to be seated. Each time, club workers ordered them to leave.

The first groups of airmen left quietly. Yet as more entered, military policemen grew agitated. They arrested black officers for disobeying orders. Groups of officers, undefeated, continued to stroll into the club. "When it was number 60 or 61, it was my turn," said Terry. "So I went, and when I got down there, they said, 'You can't come in.'"[14]

Terry and Young called reporters to tell them what had happened. The event became known as the Freeman Field Incident. Some Americans protested the treatment of the black officers. Top officials interviewed dozens of witnesses. They released most of the arrested officers. But the military remained segregated.

Months later, World War II ended. By August 1945, both Germany and Japan had surrendered to the Allies. Americans celebrated the victory. Parades wound through city streets. Brass bands led celebrations for returning soldiers. Family members proudly welcomed the Tuskegee Airmen home.

Some pilots faced a harsh adjustment to peacetime life. After years of thrilling flights, the military no longer needed them. Airmen "became elevator operators, and janitors, and porters," said pilot Charles DeBow.[15] Some struggled to find any work at all. In 1946, the Tuskegee training program closed.

Yet military rules were slowly changing. That same year, military experts met to discuss roles for black officers. Finally, in 1948, President Harry S. Truman ended segregation in the military. Tuskegee Airmen became instructors in the new U.S. Air Force. One airman, Daniel James, would become the first black four-star general.

◄ Airmen in Italy played cards in an officers' club in 1945.

Many Tuskegee-trained pilots flew in later wars. Charles McGee eagerly enlisted in the Korean War. "In May 1950, I got orders to go to the Philippines," he remembered. "On July 29, 1950, I took my first flight in a Mustang since November 1944."[16]

In later years, Tuskegee Airmen met with new Air Force members. "Everything should be done to pass [our] story to future generations," reflected pilot Ted Johnson.[17] The Tuskegee Airmen not only served during international wars. They also fought prejudice in their own country. Today, hundreds of black pilots serve in the military. Many view the Tuskegee Airmen as heroes.

"The Tuskegee Airmen served a nation not willing to serve them. Their legacy made my rise in the military possible. I stood on their shoulders. They made America better for all of us."

—*General Colin Powell, U.S. Secretary of State from 2001 to 2005*[18]

Several Tuskegee Airmen pilots and others connected with ▶ the group attended a Veterans' Day celebration in 2013.

GLOSSARY

air raids (AIR RAIDZ): During air raids, attackers drop bombs from airplanes. The Tuskegee Airmen took part in air raids over an Italian island.

bombers (BAH-merz): Bombers are airplanes that carry and drop bombs. Bombers were heavier and slower than fighter planes.

cadets (kuh-DETZ): Cadets are students in a military program. Cadets at the Tuskegee Institute studied science and airplane equipment.

combat (KOM-bat): Combat is fighting between armed forces. Soldiers are in combat against the enemy during a war.

escorting (es-KAWRT-ing): Escorting means protecting a person or thing by traveling together. By escorting bomber planes, the Tuskegee Airmen protected these vehicles from attacks.

formation (for-MAY-shun): A formation is a structure or pattern. Pilots often flew in formation, with each plane flying in a certain position near the others.

prejudice (PREH-juh-diss): Prejudice is an unfair way of thinking about a group of people. The Tuskegee Airmen often faced prejudice.

segregated (SEG-ri-gey-ted): When people are segregated, they are divided into groups based on their race. The military was segregated into black units and white units.

squadron (SQUA-drun): A squadron is an organized military group. An Air Force squadron includes pilots, commanders, and mechanics.

sweeps (SWEEPS): Sweeps are detailed searches of an area to look for something. Pilots often made sweeps of areas, looking for enemy locations and equipment.

SOURCE NOTES

1. "Found in the Archives: First Lady Eleanor Roosevelt and 'Chief' Charles Alfred Anderson, 1941." *In Roosevelt History*. Franklin D. Roosevelt Presidential Library and Museum, 17 Nov. 2011. Web. 25 Jul. 2015.

2. Charles W. Dryden. *A-Train: Memoirs of a Tuskegee Airman*. Tuscaloosa, AL: U of Arizona P, 2002. Print. 48.

3. Randy Roughton. "Tuskegee Airmen: Turning Dreams into Reality." *U.S. Air Force*. U.S. Air Force, 11 Feb. 2014. Web. 25 Jul. 2015.

4. Charles W. Dryden. 63.

5. Marlow Stern. "Dr. Roscoe Brown, A Real-Life Tuskegee Airman, Tells His 'Red Tails' Story." *The Daily Beast*. The Daily Beast Company LLC, 18 Jan. 2011. Web. 25 Jul. 2015.

6. Betty Kaplan Gubert, Miriam Sawyer, and Caroline M. Fannin. "Robert W. Deiz." *The African American Experience*. Greenwood Publishing Group, n.d. Web. 25 Jul. 2015.

7. J. Todd Moye. *Freedom Flyers: The Tuskegee Airmen* of World War II. New York: Oxford UP, 2010. Print. 96–97.

8. J. Todd Moye. 98.

9. "Tuskegee Airmen Fly First Mission by Black Pilots." *History.com*. A&E Television Networks, LLC, n.d. Web. 25 Jul. 2015.

10. Marlow Stern. 18 Jan. 2011.

11. Lynn Homan and Thomas Reilly. *Black Knights: The Story of the Tuskegee Airmen*. Gretna, LA: Pelican, 2001. Print. 91.

12. Betty Kaplan Gubert, Miriam Sawyer, and Caroline M. Fannin. *Distinguished African Americans in Aviation and Space Science*. Santa Barbara, CA: Greenwood, 2002. Print. 149.

13. "Aviation History: Interview with Tuskegee Airman Charles McGee." *HistoryNet*. HistoryNet, LLC, n.d. Web. 25 Jul. 2015.

14. "Freeman Field Mutiny." *Redtail.org*. CAF Red Tail Squadron, n.d. Web. 25 Jul. 2015.

15. Charles DeBow. "I Got Wings." *National Black Chamber of Commerce*. National Black Chamber of Commerce, n.d. Web. 25 Jul. 2015.

16. "Aviation History: Interview with Tuskegee Airman Charles McGee." n.d.

17. "Tuskegee Airmen Suit Up, Head to Iraq." *USA Today*. Gannett Information Network, 22 Oct. 2005. Web. 25 Jul. 2015.

18. "Their Legacy." *Redtail.org*. CAF Red Tail Squadron, n.d. Web. 25 Jul. 2015.

TO LEARN MORE

Books

Adams, Simon. *World War II*. New York: DK Publishing, 2014.

Graham, Ian. *You Wouldn't Want to Be a World War II Pilot!: Air Battles You Might Not Survive*. New York: Franklin Watts, 2009.

Shea, John M. *Heroes of Black History: The Tuskegee Airmen*. New York: Gareth Stevens, 2015.

Web Sites

Visit our Web site for links about the Tuskegee Airmen: childsworld.com/links

Note to Parents, Teachers, and Librarians: We routinely verify our Web links to make sure they are safe and active sites. So encourage your readers to check them out!

INDEX